Bygone Penzance
and Newlyn

PENZANCE.

The name 'Pen-Sans', meaning 'holy head', originally refer-
red to the former headland on the site of the present
Battery Rocks, on which stood the tiny chapel of St
Anthony. In considering a fitting motif for their Seal in
1614, townsfolk opted for the punning device of St John
the Baptist's 'holy head' on a charger. (Reproduced by
courtesy of Penzance Town Council.)

Bygone PENZANCE and NEWLYN

Sheila Bird

Phillimore

1987

Published by
PHILLIMORE & CO. LTD.,
Shopwyke Hall, Chichester, Sussex, England

© Sheila Bird, 1987

ISBN 0 85033 633 3

Printed and bound in Great Britain by
BIDDLES LTD.
Guildford and King's Lynn

To the seafaring fraternity

List of Illustrations

Acknowledgements

In compiling *Bygone Penzance and Newlyn*, I should like to thank the many people who have helped to make it such an interesting and enjoyable project. In particular Jonathan Holmes, John Laity, Eddie Richards, Jacqui Ramsey, Lesley Byrne, Ben Batten, Jane Stephen, Myfanwy Simpson (née Bofanko), Leen Meyer, John Bennetts, John Peak, Fred Peak, John Corin, Ken Thomas and the R.N.L.I. I am indebted to Mrs. B. J. Milner for her help in supplying pictures, and to the Richards family, photographers of Penzance.

As with the publication of *Bygone Falmouth* and *Bygone Truro*, I am again indebted to Brian Errington for his high quality photographic work, to Terry Barham, the late Fisher Barham and Gloria Parker; to Terry Knight and the staff of the Cornwall Local Studies Library, Redruth, for all their cheerful help and interest; to the County Council's library in Morrab Road, the Royal Geological Society of Cornwall, Penzance Town Council, Penlee House Museum and the Penzance Library, Morrab House, for help in research, and for allowing me to draw on their fine selection of old photographs.

For the use of photographs I am indebted to Penlee House Museum for numbers 2, 3, 5, 9, 14, 15, 19, 20, 22, 34, 35, 36, 39, 40, 41, 43, 45, 49, 50, 51, 52, 58, 66, 68, 81, 82, 85, 87, 88, 90, 94, 95, 108, 109, 112, 113, 114, 122, 123, 125, 127, 129, 134, 136, 138, 146, 147, 150 and the frontispiece; to the Penzance Library, Morrab House, for numbers 12, 18, 21, 31, 32, 37, 38, 42, 55, 59, 60, 61, 62, 63, 64, 91, 92, 98, 99, 105, 106, 107, 110, 117, 119, 132, 135, 140, 142, 143, 144, 148, 149, 151, 153; to the Local Studies, Redruth, for numbers 1, 4, 11, 13, 128, 139, 145; to Fisher Barham for numbers 23, 28, 152; to Jonathan Holmes for numbers 6 and 120; to Fred and John Peak for number 16; to Jane Stephen and Penzance Library for number 118; to Mrs. B. J. Milner for numbers 57 and 97; to Penzance Town Council for permission to reproduce number 154; to C. T. Bird for number 33. Other photographs are from the author's own collection.

Early Days around Mount's Bay

The pleasing northern shoreline of Mount's Bay, dominated by the romantic eminence of St Michael's Mount and sheltered by a hinterland rich in archaeological remains, is steeped in colourful legend and history. The Mount is thought to be the 'island off Britain called Ictis', documented by the Sicilian Greek historian Diodorus in the early part of the first century A.D. as exporting tin to the Mediterranean before the birth of Christ.

Market Jew, on the mainland just across the Causeway and better known today as Marazion, had capitalised on the tin trade and the religious importance of the Mount to become an established trading centre when Penzance was a mere cluster of fishermen's dwellings around a tiny chapel on a headland which has long since eroded away. Mousehole, on the western shores, with a south pier dating from A.D. 400, was a larger, more flourishing port than Penzance in earlier times. The first tangible reference to Penzance occurs in 1284. In 1435 the Bishop of Exeter issued a special appeal for contributions towards 'the repairing and maintaining of a certain quay or jetty at Newlyn in the Parish of Paul'. The old quay offered shelter to a limited number of small boats but, until 1885, larger vessels relying on shelter from the headland were vulnerable to south and south-easterly gales. Penzance harbour was originally built to accommodate fishing vessels but, by medieval times, it was exporting smoked pilchards to the Mediterranean and importing salt as a preservative.

* * * * *

Folk living around the shores of Mount's Bay have long been accustomed to fluctuating fortunes and devastating blows of fate ranging from seaward invasions to recurring pestilence and storm. Carew, the early historian, suggested that they may have been rather too resigned in their attitude to disaster, giving credence to the prophetic rhyme that 'Strangers would land on the rocks of Merlin, who would burn Paul's church, Penzance and Newlyn'. In 1595, after the Armada, the Spaniards brought this prophecy to fruition when they landed at Mousehole, catching the terrified inhabitants completely by surprise. Having destroyed the village, set Paul church ablaze and then attacked Newlyn, they turned their fiery attentions to Penzance and, meeting scant opposition, they razed it to the ground. It was only after the damage had been inflicted that the brave Sir Francis Godolphin managed to muster sufficient local military power and seaward reinforcements to send the marauders scuttling back to their ships. Few buildings survived this onslaught. In 1646 staunchly Royalist Penzance suffered another devastating attack, this time from Fairfax's army, thereby paying a very high price for its loyalty. When war with Spain broke out in 1739, townsfolk, aware of their previous vulnerability, emplaced guns on the strategic site of the 'holy headland' where that early chapel of St Anthony once stood; it was thereafter known as Battery Rocks.

In 1614, less than twenty years after the devastating Spanish attacks, Penzance had recovered sufficiently to be granted borough status by James I. It went on to develop its trading potential by land and sea, ousting Marazion as the region's principal market. A market house was erected at the top of Market Jew Street in an area which had traditionally been the busy hub of social life, with itinerant traders, farmers and fisherfolk setting up their stalls in the open air and crying their wares. In 1663 Penzance received a further boost by being chosen as a coinage town, which meant that all the tin produced in the area had to be brought here for testing, with dues payable by the smelters. The harbour thrived on the export of tin, and the corporation derived a healthy income from its harbour, markets and fairs. But there was a setback in the reign of James II when the Charter, which was perfectly in order, was questioned. Restoring the status quo cost the townsfolk dearly and added to the unpopularity of the king. This gave rise to the protest song and local anthem 'Trelawny', which has been revised in more recent times to plead causes in the face of subsequent bureaucratic injustices. There was a further setback at the beginning of the 18th century when the town temporarily lost its Charter.

Evidence of Christianity in the locality dates from the 10th century, although it had been established in Cornwall 500 years earlier. Madron was the mother Church but as Penzance expanded, a chapel of ease was established in the town for practical reasons. The ancient chapel of St Anthony, which served the spiritual needs of fisherfolk, later functioned as a fish cellar, and a badly mutilated cross salvaged from its fabric at a later date was placed in the present St Mary's churchyard. John Wesley and his brother Charles, who were around Penzance with their distinctive brand of religious fervour in the 1740s, were regarded as a threat by the vicar of Madron. Unabashed, Wesley carried on preaching, commiserating with the flock about their minister and recalling rather grandly in his journal, 'I cried to a mixed multitude of wakened and unawakened sinners near Penzance ...' Methodism and its splinter sects took root here as did a multiplicity of other denominations. In the last century fervently religious fishermen of Newlyn, who abstained from fishing on the Sabbath, were overcome with righteous indignation when east coast fishermen poached their waters as they knelt in prayer, thereby monopolising the Monday market. This erupted into the Newlyn Riots in May and June 1896.

During the first part of the 18th century the militia was called in when miners, angry about the high price of corn, converged on Penzance. A Penzance agent, appealing for reinforcements later that century, recorded that 'the coasts here swarm with smugglers'. Wheel tracks in the rocks, caverns, secret tunnels and concealed cellars tell a tale of this illicit growth industry in which all sections of society were involved. In 1769 the Mayor of Penzance, no less, was 'bound over in a large sum not to again be guilty of smuggling'.

In the course of day-to-day life petty offenders were placed in the pillory or stocks to be pelted with garbage, or whipped through the streets. During the 18th century a pillory stood close to the debtors' prison in the stable yard of the former *Shoulder of Mutton Inn* at the Greenmarket. The four constables who patrolled the streets were able to take refuge from the weather in little sentry-type boxes placed around the town. Intriguingly, a 'scold's bridle', used for curbing nagging female tongues, was acquired by the corporation at that time. The town's two prisons, condemned as being cramped, dark, foul and rat infested, were replaced in 1826 by another, in St Clare Street, where the treadmill and bread and water diet were seen as enlighted forms of treatment for rebellious inmates. Almshouses built by Francis Buller in 1660 were later used as a Poor House.

Although life was hard, ordinary folk had long demonstrated their ability to cast care aside and make merry at festivals and fairs with music, dancing and the traditional burning of tar barrels. Christmas was a time for carol singing and dancing, while May Day was heralded by excited children rushing around the streets at dawn, blaring away on discordant tin horns. In rural parts there was an old farmhouse custom of suspending special saffron and currant hot cross buns from the rafters each year to ward off bad luck. The Midsummer Eve celebrations, probably deriving from the ancient summer solstice, involved bonfires on the hillsides and blazing tar barrels in the candlelit streets. Little girls, dressed in white and garlanded with flowers or leaves, emerged into doorways as the festivities began. There were torchlit processions through the streets, and the celebrations gathered momentum as lasses and lads ran around the town playing a chain dance called 'thread the needle'. Until the end of the last century a mock mayor was elected in the Greenmarket, giving townsfolk who had enjoyed a drink or two the chance to say what was on their mind. Any overexuberance was cooled as safety hoses doused the glowing tar barrels, along with anything else that happened to be in the way. The decline of these colourful traditions was hastened by the fire insurance companies disclaiming responsibility for mishaps. On Midsummer Day the crowds converged on the Quay Fair. The Corpus Christi Fair numbered among its attractions theatrical performances, peep shows, menageries, boxing, conjuring, roundabouts and swings, as well as the opportunity to gape at freaks, drink intoxicating liquor or be tempted by a mouth-watering display of goodies to eat. Circuses and travelling players also visited Penzance, while cock fighting and wrestling contests were followed with enthusiasm by all sections of society.

These were welcome diversions from the hard grind of daily life. In the last century men in the area were employed in tanning, smelting, brewing and other manufacturing, service and maritime trades. The womenfolk had a full-time task looking after their large families, carrying water, washing, sewing, ironing, cleaning and cooking. During the season they prepared salted fish in earthenware containers to help them survive the difficult winter months. Everyday fare consisted mainly of stews, fish, potatoes and other vegetables, bread and milk. Pies, pasties and cakes were taken to the local bakehouse to be cooked.

As a prosperous community, Penzance was favoured by the Cornish gentry many of whom took up residence here in the 18th century. Girls from the farming and mining areas, who felt that life was passing them by, welcomed the chance to work as servants in Penzance. It became a place of culture with book clubs, libraries, theatres, concert rooms, an art school and art gallery. Two particularly distinctive institutions are the Royal Geological Society of Cornwall, founded in 1814 by Dr. Paris, a local practitioner who later became president of the Royal College of Surgeons, and the Morrab Library, aptly described by Sir Arthur Quiller Couch as 'a library in a garden'. Supported by noteworthy benefactors, it has built up a fascinating collection of rare books, first editions and Cornish books, earning an international reputation. This cultural background has attracted leading figures in the world of science and the arts. Among the notable people to be connected with

Penzance are Edward Pellew, who ran away to sea as a child, achieved fame and glory and was created a baronet, Davies Gilbert, and the multi-talented Sir Humphry Davy, who became one of the greatest figures of the scientific world and is particularly remembered for his invention of the miners' safety lamp.

Davies Gilbert and Sir Humphry Davy, who were both elected presidents of the Royal Society, attended the Grammar School in Penzance, which has since closed. There was a National School for girls and another for boys, and in 1909 Penzance County School for Boys was built. This was later renamed the Humphry Davy School, in honour of the town's most illustrious son. Former pupils of the West Cornwall School remember walking in sedate crocodile formation in their brown and cream uniforms to the Methodist church in Chapel Street on Sundays, and their rivalry with St Clare's Church of England boarding school.

In Napoleonic times fashionable folk who formerly travelled to Europe began to look nearer home and were attracted to Penzance with its mild, equable climate, attractive coastline, luxuriant vegetation and slightly Continental flavour. Physicians extolled the virtues of the resort's sea air and sea water. The arrival of the West Cornwall railway in 1852 and the link with London when Brunel's bridge opened at Saltash in 1859 put Penzance firmly on the map.

Towards the end of the last century neighbouring Newlyn, only a mile distant but totally different in spirit with its quaint courts and alleyways and colourful fisherfolk, became the focus of artists who were collectively known as the Newlyn School. Today exhibitions of their work arouse great interest and their paintings command high prices. Local youths were employed in copper repoussé work in a former fish curing cellar on the harbourside, and the Newlyn artists assisted with the designs.

A guidebook of 1865 enthused 'Few spectacles are more pleasing than that which is so often presented by this beautiful bay, when its fishing fleet has assembled, equipped and ready for sea, or, with hull and sail illuminated by a setting sun, is leaving the shore in a line extending seaward as far as the eye can reach'. While some were attracted to the area, others, who had perhaps grown accustomed to its charms, set their sights on adventure overseas. After reputedly dreaming up the scheme in the *Star Inn* at Penzance, seven local fishermen, attracted by the excitement of the Australian gold rush but unable to afford the steamship fares, set sail from Newlyn in their 37-foot, partly-decked mackerel boat *Mystery* in 1854, cheered off by crowds of well wishers lining the shore. It was a feat of seamanship unparalleled at the time. Ocean-going vessels were built in Penzance throughout the 19th century and several were constructed for the Penzance Shipping Company, which had been set up by a consortium of local merchants in 1809 to trade direct with London. Vessels of other companies traded with Bristol and Plymouth as well as London. Penzance has always been the main contender as the mainland port for the Isles of Scilly, supplying them with essential goods and exporting their early flowers and vegetables. In the middle of the last century emigrant ships left Penzance and Newlyn for the New World.

Penzance, famed for its agreeable climate, has suffered some devastating storms, particularly in the latter part of the last century. In the Great Blizzard of 1891 hedges, farm animals, lanes and streets disappeared beneath a great depth of snow. Farms and villages were cut off and the temperatures were so low that ships lost their bearings.

Mount's Bay has always been notorious for shipwrecks, particularly when the wind is in the south and east and ships may be driven into rocks or shallows. Traditionally rescues have been carried out by fishermen and boatmen with a good knowledge of local conditions, and many heroic rescues have been carried out by pilot gigs. A lifeboat of north country design, financed by the Corporation of Lloyds and local subscribers, was introduced in 1803, but appears to have remained unused, probably because the seafarers preferred to tackle difficult conditions in their own familiar craft. The folk of Penzance were prompt to support the Royal National Institution for the Preservation of Life from Shipwreck which was established in 1824, and a lifeboat of the 'Plenty' style arrived in 1826. This was followed by a succession of Peake, Self Righting and Watson lifeboats operating from stations at the western end of the Promenade and Wharf Road before the move to Penlee in 1913. Various lifeboats operated from here throughout the Second World War, and the service was called upon frequently. A Tidal Observatory was set up on the end of Newlyn's South Pier in April 1915 when the pier was extended. It remains of worldwide importance, measuring land and tidal movements, mean sea levels, temperatures and other data.

The weather was exceptionally mild throughout the festive season in 1913. Folk in hospital and in the workhouse had enjoyed traditional Christmas fare and entertainments and the New Year started promisingly around Mount's Bay with a bumper crop of early spring flowers. However, war was on the way. H.M.S. *Africa* visited Penzance in June 1914 and made 'a very pleasant connection with the town'. Her sister ships *Orion* and *Monarch*, of the latest Dreadnought type, arrived decorated for the King's birthday celebrations. Further excitement came in from the sea that summer when the Falmouth tug *Victor* brought a motley assortment of East European migrants ashore from the wreck of the *Gothland*. In July reservists were summoned to the naval base at Portsmouth, and on 6 August 1914 confirmed the situation that everyone feared by announcing: 'Europe at War'.

There was a flurry of local activity as more reservists were called up, and there was a big recruitment drive. German aliens were taken into custody at Chyandour and searched for weapons, but none were found. A number of these prisoners took part in a frantic but abortive rescue bid to save a drowning woman, some of them remaining in the water for many hours. The railway station became the scene of many stirring, stiff-upper-lip, patriotic departures with military music and hearty cheers. The port of Penzance became an auxiliary naval base and Holman's offices were used as the regional headquarters for naval personnel, with the entire workforce and facilities harnessed for the war effort. At the end of the war the firm was recompensed for resultant wear and tear. Women and girls were put to agricultural work. Hampers of vegetables were sent to sailors and weekly consignments of eggs were dispatched to the National Egg Collection for distribution to the wounded in hospital. Medicinal herbs were grown. Girl Guides collected silver paper and waste paper to boost the war effort and a number of war relief funds were set up. As Belgian orphans arrived in Penzance, local children were urged to accept them into their games and make them feel at home. But even wartime has its moments of comedy. A Belgian artist who was the guest of the local committee was happily sketching a picturesque vessel (which happened to be a government trawler) in Newlyn harbour, when a pistol was pointed at his head and he was arrested as a spy! The surprised prisoner was promptly marched off to the vicarage where his innocence was established. It transpired that he had been given special permission to paint around the streets and harbour.

The authorities could not afford to take chances when it came to the question of security. German submarines lurking in Mount's Bay caused a number of incidents involving convoys, steamships and fishing vessels between here and the Scillies, and east-country steam drifters in deep waters in exposed situations needed patrol protection. In 1915 a British warship arrested a three-masted schooner flying a French flag, which was loaded with petroleum casks and suspected of supplying fuel to the Germans. The formidable armed guard which went aboard to investigate was met by a cool captain and his equally nonchalant crew, who had no identity papers at all.

There was tremendous relief when peace came at last, and it was anticipated that the Christmas of 1918 would long be remembered as the 'Peace Christmas'. For nothing like this could ever happen again, could it? The Union flag was much in evidence on Armistice Day and Mount's Bay re-echoed to a strident cacophony of ships' sirens. To mark the end of the conflict there were civic processions, entertainments for the children and dancing along the seafront. Later an ex-German submarine at Penzance was opened to the public, who were asked not to help themselves to souvenirs. At a meeting held in the Guildhall it was decided to erect a war memorial, in the form of an obelisk, clearly inscribed with the names of those who had fallen, and Battery Rocks, the site of the early settlement which evolved into Penzance, was chosen for its prominent position. Newlyn and the surrounding villages similarly honoured their dead. At Newlyn a stone column above the old slipway was erected in memory of Louisa A. M. McGrigor, who died on active service in 1917.

After the war the motorised bus service improved links with the outlying villages. As well as benefiting local folk, it enabled visitors who had arrived by train to use Penzance as a convenient centre for touring. Although recognised as a resort, Penzance never sacrificed itself to tourism, and has always remained a bustling market town and port.

The people of Newlyn, a tough, proud and independent breed, were outraged when cottages which had been the homes of fisherfolk for generations were condemned as unfit for habitation by Penzance Town Council in the late 1930s. For them council houses up on the hill were no substitute for their traditional homes, handy for their boats and where they could dry and mend their nets. Angry protest meetings were held in the hope of getting the decision reversed, but the council steadfastly refused to give way. Deciding to appeal to higher authority, the fishermen set sail for Westminster in the long liner *Rosebud* and, amidst great publicity, presented their petition at the Houses of Parliament. The coming of the Second World War probably helped to halt the clearance scheme. Ironically, homes left empty for compulsory demolition were to be used for housing Belgian refugees during the war.

On Thursday 7 September 1939 *The Cornishman & Cornish Telegraph* carried a headline with a chillingly familiar ring about it, 'Outbreak of European War', and told of lights going out in Europe and skies darkening with strife. Suddenly everyday life took on an unfamiliar aspect as the municipal buildings and other establishments were sandbagged and pavements were edged with white lines. Street lighting was dispensed with for the duration of the war, householders blacked out their homes, shops and cinemas were darkened and buses with curtained windows and dipped headlights crept eerily through the night-time streets. An emergency timetable was put into operation by the G.W.R. A Food Control Committee was set up in Penzance, where there were ongoing problems about the supply and price of meat. The port of Newlyn was taken over by a Fish Controller who fixed the prices. During the early years of the war fishing vessels regularly returned to Newlyn and Mousehole laden with heavy, mixed catches. The Admiralty reinforced the minesweeper flotillas by acquiring trawlers and drifters, and appealed for experienced volunteers to man them. A call went out for able-bodied men to meet the recruitment crisis. Within the first few days of the war three Penzance men were killed when H.M.S. *Courageous*, with her escort in attendance, was struck by an enemy submarine. German bombers had been wreaking havoc over England, but Cornwall was generally regarded by city dwellers as a place of refuge and advertisements in the newspapers drew attention to the pleasures of holidaying the in the Beautiful Scillies.

As early as 1938 the Borough of Penzance had organised the ARP service into groups G and H. With the onset of war full-scale anti-aircraft practices were carried out by the combined ARP services with fire fighters, decontamination squads, rescue parties and first aid sections being put through their paces. Householders peered uneasily from behind their curtains as fire engines, trailer pumps and ambulances rumbled heavily through the dawn streets.

The exhibition of paintings went ahead as usual in 1939 – as it did throughout the war – with Stanhope Forbes pointing out that 'these are difficult times for all of us, but they fall particularly hard upon artists'. He added, 'It is an achievement to hold an exhibition at all, and we feel it also to be a kind of manifesto of sanity and idealism'. It was government policy to present the censored news in an optimistic way to keep morale high. There were concert parties and the Penzance Pavilion provided light-hearted entertainment designed to beat the blackout blues. The cinema allowed temporary escape from the problems of reality, while cricket, rugby, football, boxing and other sports provided a means of letting off steam. The Bishop of Truro, preaching at St John's church, spoke of the importance of keeping in touch with God.

A Services Christmas Fund was set up early in the war to send hundreds of parcels and postal orders to the lads overseas, to brighten up the festive season. Just before the first wartime Christmas, three ships of the British Merchant Marine were attacked by a U-boat at very short range off Land's End. The unarmed *Baharistan* overcame the attack by skilful navigation and was able to anchor in the safety of Mount's Bay, a feat for which the skipper was awarded the O.B.E. The Newlyn fishing boat *Peel Castle* netted more than she bargained for when an unidentified submerged object carried away her entire tackle as she fished off Polperro. Another mystery surrounded a lifeboat found empty and devoid of paddles, tiller or rudder, and bearing the name *Java*. She was found close to wreckage south of the Lowlee Buoy in 1940, and towed into Newlyn harbour by the trawler *Efficient*. St Michael's Mount, which had always formed a natural protective fortress for the bay, had three blockhouses constructed at its base as a defence against German U-boats. On one occasion the village was machine gunned by enemy aircraft, but there were no casualties.

Gas masks were issued for children in March 1940, with helmets and respirators for younger children, and the Penzance area prepared itself for the 2,500 evacuees it had been allotted. One small Cockney boy who had never before seen the sea was heard to remark after the official welcoming of the evacuees from London, 'Cor blimey', I ain't never seen so much blooming water in all me blooming life'. After being taken to reception centres and plied with refreshments, the children were distributed to homes and hostels around the area. They were boisterous and volunteers were sought to keep them amused with games and activities.

There have always been strong bonds within the fishing community, and when Belgian refugees, including fishermen's families, arrived in Newlyn, Mr. B. D. Stevenson, who had previously worked with some of them and spoke Belgian, was instrumental in getting them housed in empty fishermen's cottages. Well wishers donated furniture. In addition to this, Penzance became the receiving centre for the children of wealthy Dutch families, who became known as 'War Children'.

Irresponsible people who flouted the blackout regulations were taken to task. Most of the bombing was carried out at night, with senior pupils of the Humphry Davy School helping out with firewatching. The Western Union Cable Office (now Alverton Court) was sandbagged and guarded by armed police. Just after Dunkirque the Royal Inniskellin Fusiliers, who were briefly stationed in Penzance, patrolled the streets at night with searchlights and machine guns, challenging anyone who appeared to be loitering with intent. The emergency services were regularly put through their paces, but the real test for the firefighters came with a civilian blaze in Trouncen's timber yard in New Street. Penzance fire brigade, ably supported by men of the auxiliary fire service, prevented the fire from spreading to the back of the *Union Hotel*. There was a slight mishap when P.C. Toms was struck full in the face by a jet of water and had to be assisted from the scene, and another when the Chief Constable was caught squarely in the back of the neck by another erring jet, much to the merriment of the onlookers. Eight families were evacuated when a big fire destroyed Taylor's Garage in Coinagehall Street in 1944, and English and American soldiers billeted nearby retrieved bedding and furniture, and discouraged civilians from entering the area.

The Americans, who were generous and well liked, joined in enthusiastically with morale-boosting activities and impressed everybody with their enormous sousaphones. Their headquarters were at the gracious building now known as Camelot where, until recently, top-floor rooms still bore the labels 'Cell 1' and 'Cell 2'. Their PX Club was in Causewayhead.

In June 1944 local people watched as support ships from South Wales formed a line, silhouetted along the horizon, and the tension mounted in readiness for the D-Day landings. The departure of the Americans left a void, but there was excitement when a BBC van arrived to record an edition of that favourite wartime show, 'Workers' Playtime', from St John's Hall. Sylvia Handel and Jack Warner provided sweetness and laughter, while the dashing, handsome commentator Bill Gates added a touch of sophistication, uttering those immortal lines, 'And this is Bill Gates wishing you luck, war workers ...', as he did on the radio every week. Fund-raising events, which did much for wartime social life as well as supporting the war effort, continued with 'Salute the Soldier Week', when a miniature paratroop cycle headed the procession of the defence services and allied units.

By the beginning of 1945 thoughts were turning to such issues as the homecoming of the troops, the unsatisfactory housing situation, the prospects for post-war industry and the future of cricket in West Cornwall. Newlyn fishermen pressed the government for the release of their boats, so that they could have them reconditioned as soon as possible and regain their source of livelihood.

V.E. Day on 8 June 1945 saw the streets of Penzance, Newlyn and surrounding villages bedecked with flags and bunting. Thankfulness and relief were tempered with concern for those who fought on, and sadness for those who would never return. Some people were confused as to whether or not to turn up for work on such an auspicious day, and uncertain about the blackout situation. But at 3.00 p.m. all radios were tuned in to the Prime Minister's broadcast. Thanksgiving services were held and church bells re-echoed across the meadows and the bay. Revellers flocked along the seafront and, rather incongruously, a police car toured the area warning people not to take down or destroy their blackout material. There were street parties, fancy-dress parades and races. That night the post office choir gave a memorable performance of Kipling's 'Recessional' at the ATC headquarters in Penzance, timed to coincide with the European cease-fire order at midnight. The week of celebrations was rounded off the following Sunday with a day of thanksgiving and prayer, and the blackout restrictions were finally lifted.

The Plates

Early Days

1. St Michael's Mount and Marazion, *c.*1860, from an engraving by William Willis. In former times St Michael's Mount and Marazion were the focus of religious, commercial and military life around Mount's Bay, the Mount forming a natural defence. Penzance was to usurp Marazion as the area's trading centre, but the Mount, steeped in colourful romance and history, still plays host to royal visitors and attracts many tourists.

2. St Michael's Mount as shown in an engraving of 1810. The Mount was anciently known as *Ictis*. According to legend the monastery marks the spot where the Archangel Michael appeared to some humble fishermen. Legend also has it that Joseph of Arimathea traded with Market Jew (Marazion) for tin. The Celtic name for the Mount was 'The Hoar Rock in the Wood'.

3. At exceptionally low tide evidence of a submerged forest, carbon dated by Sir Gavin de Beer around 1700 B.C., is exposed between Marazion and Penzance and near Wherrytown.

4. Mount's Bay from Gulval Carn, from an engraving by William Willis, *c*.1860. According to legend, the lost, idyllic land of Lyonesse lies just beyond the horizon, and the bells of the submerged churches are said to be heard on very still days.

5. Penzance foreshore from the west, as it looked in the last century, with the distinctive, whitewashed spire of old St Mary's creating a navigational landmark. Pen-Sans originated as a cluster of fisherfolk's dwellings around the ancient chapel of St Anthony on the headland, now eroded, and known as Battery Rocks (seen here, centre right).

6. Fishing fleet in Mount's Bay. From medieval times smoked pilchards were exported to the Mediterranean and salt was imported from France. In the 17th century Penzance was described by Daniel Defoe as 'a place of good business, well built and populous, having a good trade and a great many ships belonging to it'.

7. The Greenmarket, seen here in 1829, where petty offenders were placed in the pillory in the 18th century, was originally a cattle market. Fairs, traditionally set up here, were very popular, but caused nearby householders to complain of the noise, particularly the roaring of the caged wild animals.

8. The Celtic cross, inscribed *Hic Procumbant Corpora Piorum* and *Regis Ricati Crux* (the cross of King Ricatus), stood in the Bullock Market, now the Green Market, in the last century, where farmers found it useful for tethering animals. It variously stood at the bottom of Causewayhead, outside the Market House, in Morrab Gardens, and now stands outside Penlee Museum.

9. St Mary's chapel, 1832. The chapel was damaged during the Spanish attack of 1595, but repairs and subsequent additions were made in the 17th century. At that time men and women were segregated during the services. The last service was preached here on 29 July 1832, just before its demolition.

10. The former Market House, c.1833, was built on a site traditionally used for markets and fairs. It was constructed in 1614 when Penzance became a borough. It was demolished in the mid-1830s to make way for the present Market House.

11. (*above*) An engraving by William Willis, *c*.1860, which shows the original Penzance railway terminus and the harbour beyond. The coming of the railway in 1852 effectively put Penzance on the map. A road was later constructed from the docks, across Ross Bridge and along the waterfront to connect with the station. A large section of the harbour was filled in to create a car park.

12. (*opposite above*) Wherrytown, where there were once sandy towans and a rope walk, derives its name from this old wherry mine, situated below an off-shore reef. It was powered by an engine on land, and was a great feat of engineering. However it did not pay and, despite several attempts to revive the industry, it closed down in 1838.

13. (*opposite below*) Plans to create a port at the hauntingly beautiful Lamorna Cove proved abortive, but granite shipped from the quarries here was used in the construction of the Thames Embankment. The artist Lamorna Birch so loved the place that he made his home here. The description 'Lamorna' Birch distinguished him from another artist with the same surname. This engraving by William Willis dates from *c*.1860.

Trade and Industry

14. (*opposite above*) The Serpentine Works at Wherrytown, erected in 1854 on the site of the present Bolitho Gardens, fashioned functional objects and ornaments from highly-polished serpentine stone from the Lizard. This building served a variety of purposes before being demolished in 1916.

15. (*opposite below*) Messrs. Bolitho & Company's Smelting Works at Chyandour. In 1883 the tin smelting works employed about 15 men earning an average of 19s. a week. It closed in 1912, having functioned for almost two hundred years.

16. (*above*) John Peak set up his business as a picture frame maker and house decorator in Causewayhead in 1882. The service covered a wide area, with equipment transported in a two-wheeled handcart. By the turn of the century there were 30 workmen, who lodged here during the week. This photograph shows employees Tommy Nicholls and Charlie Rowe in the 1920s.

17. (*below*) Daffodil fields around Gulval in the 1920s. 'The Golden Mile' was the popular name given to this fertile agricultural belt with a favoured climate, where early broccoli and daffodils thrive. Marazion Marsh, running parallel with the coast, once provided a fine habitat for plants and birds, and was the particular delight of botanists and artists.

18. A picturesque
scene as early
potatoes, destined
for the London
markets, are harves-
ted close to the
shores of Mount's
Bay about 1935. In
earlier days whole
families worked in
the fields, tilling by
spade to plant early
vegetables. In spring-
time the air was
touched with the
delicate fragrance
of flowers. Decaying
seaweed, used as a
fertiliser, created
another evocative
aroma.

Trade by Water

19. (*opposite above*) A very early picture of the Penzance waterfront, *c.*1860, as it looked before the construction of Ross Bridge, Wharf Road and the car park. The barge seen here carried stone used in the construction of Wolf Rock Lighthouse.

20. (*opposite below*) Penzance waterfront, seen from almost the same position after the construction of Ross Bridge and Wharf Road, and photographed around the turn of the century.

21. (*above*) Penzance Harbour in 1869. From 1825 until 1859 a packet service operated between Penzance and the Scillies using such vessels as *Cherub*, *Lord Wellington*, *Lionesse* and *Ariadne*.

22. (*below*) Penzance docks, showing the old dock gates and Ross Bridge, *c.*1890. Ross Bridge, a swing bridge carrying a road between the floating dock and the railway station, was named after Charles Campbell Ross, who distinguished himself by being five times mayor of Penzance. The bridge and these dock gates were replaced in 1981.

23. Low tide, as construction work is carried out on the Dock Basin at Penzance in 1881. Beyond is Messrs. Mathews & Company, ship and boat builders, who owned the dry dock. Sail lofts, rope walks, timber yards, anchor forges and chandleries line the waterfront.

24.   A view across the rooftops to Newlyn Harbour, showing North and South Pier, with fishing luggers beyond, *c.*1895. The South Pier (right), constructed on a rock, was completed in 1887. The North Pier was completed the following year and further improved between 1891 and 1893. This offered shelter and deep water berths to vessels which had previously relied on shelter from the headland.

25.   Packing fish at Newlyn, *c.*1895. Salted pilchards were packed in an attractive zodiac style known as 'fairmaids', a term derived from the Italian 'fermados', and pressed down very tightly. The beautifully-fashioned copper stencils used were made by the Newlyn Art Metal Industries, whose philosophy was that everyday objects should be functional and pleasing.

26. Newlyn Old Harbour. In 1435 the Bishop of Exeter had appealed 'to all who should contribute towards repairing and maintaining of a certain quay or jetty at Newlyn, in the Parish of Paul'. The old quay sheltered about forty small boats.

27. View across Newlyn Harbour showing mackerel drivers, which were about forty feet long and drove with their drift nets on the tide. The fishermen in the foreground are wearing special bowler hats known as 'mullers' which were in effect safety helmets, offering protection from spars, blocks and other occupational hazards.

28. This picturesque scene, awaiting the arrival of the catch at Newlyn, would inspire any painter. As the fish arrived there was intense activity and the harbour, quays and streets would re-echo to the sounds of hurried hoofs, the rumble of cartwheels and urgent shouts of the fish sellers.

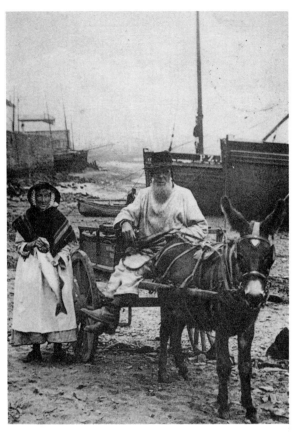

29. The catch was landed on the beach and sold to local fish hawkers who toured the area selling fish to householders from their donkey carts. Fisherfolk also set up stalls below the market place in Market Jew Street.

30. Mousehole, with a south pier dating from around A.D. 400, was formerly a place of some importance. At the turn of the century it operated a large fishing fleet and was capable of handling several cargo boats at once. Pilchards cured here gave the place a certain aura which kept visitors at bay in earlier times.

31. The gaily-coloured French crabbers which came to Newlyn for many years add a pleasing, Continental touch to the harbour in the 1920s. This picture evokes the scent of French tobacco and the kindly, well-liked fishermen who spoke no English, searched the hedgerows for snails, gathered shellfish from the rocks and wore multi-patched blue trousers and clogs.

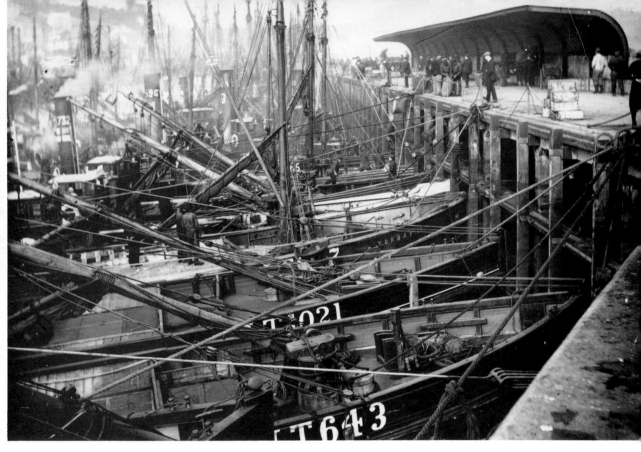

32. Lowestoft fishing vessels at Newlyn in a maze of masts, rigging, funnels and smoke, about 1930. In the last century East Coasters, who fished these waters as deeply religious Newlyners abstained from Sunday fishing, created friction which escalated into the Newlyn Riots in May and June 1896.

33. The first S.S. *Scillonian*, pictured here in 1949, was a steel-screw vessel built in Troon in 1926. She served 30 successful years on the Penzance-Scillies run. During the Second World War, the drably-painted and defensively-armed vessel became stranded on Newford Island, St Mary's, but escaped virtually intact. She was renamed Peninnis, and replaced in 1955.

Transport and Services

34. In 1743/4 Penzance Corporation purchased a fire engine and 12 leather buckets. In 1860 a new Borough Fire Brigade was formed with a Superintendent, three captains, two turncocks and nine firemen. This uniform, consisting of a loose red tunic and high, protective helmet, was introduced in 1862. In an emergency the fire bell was rung by the duty policeman.

35. Phyllis Rowe, a Penzance water carrier, delivered water from Alverton well to townsfolk for the price of 1d. or 2d. a pitcher, according to their means. She died in 1890.

36. (*above*) The watercress seller, with his pony and cart, was a familiar personality around the streets of Old Penzance. Hawkers transported a variety of commodities around the town, including sand from Hayle Towans, which was used for cleaning purposes.

37. (*below*) Horse-drawn Royal Mail vans and omnibuses outside the *First and Last Inn* in Alverton Road. Early in the last century carriages, coaches, phaetons, gigs, landaus and dog carts were built in Penzance.

38. (*overleaf*) Efficient teamwork being employed in laying electricity cables in Causewayhead. Electric light was introduced to Penzance in 1912. On the right of the picture is the Booking Office of the Union Castle Line to South Africa.

39. Champion's waggonette alongside *Queen's* around 1895. At that time only wealthy folk could afford the luxury of seaside holidays, and regular excursions ran to the Logan Rock and other places of local interest.

40. Pert horses guide the Express coach past Briton's Terrace on their journey eastwards, away from Penzance. The building on the left is now the *Pirates Hotel*, and the old Coastguard's tower is visible on the skyline.

41. The first motor bus to leave Penzance for London, on 30 September 1919. Notice the 'Leyland' nameplate over the front grille.

42. The locomotive *Penzance*, constructed at Carn Brea, seen at Penzance Station with the old signal box beyond. On 28 February 1852 she hauled a special train on a pre-opening run with invited guests from Redruth, finishing spectacularly 'over the level of Marazion Green to Chyandour, at a rate of about 30 miles an hour'.

43. The railway terminus at Penzance, showing the broad and narrow gauge tracks. The railway came in 1852 and in 1859 the opening of Brunel's Royal Albert Bridge at Saltash provided a link with London. A third rail was laid between Truro and Penzance in 1867 for mixed-gauge working, cutting out the inconvenience caused by the change of gauge at Truro.

44. This splendid terminus, designed by Lancaster Owen of the G.W.R., and described as 'one of the finest stations west of London', replaced the earlier construction in 1881. Here the photographer has captured the proud and heady days of steam with the Riviera Express.

Institutions, Events and Happenings

45. A day to remember was 7 July 1845, when Samuel Pidwell laid the foundation stone of North Pier (later renamed Albert Pier) to the firing of cannons and cheers of thousands of spectators. This was followed by the opening of the Fish Market (now demolished), refreshments for all, as befitted their class, and fishwives leading dancing through the streets.

46. Recalling the tidal wave that never was . . . In 1869 there was mounting panic over a predicted tidal wave which threatened to submerge the village at the base of the Mount. There was intense relief — and a feeling of anti-climax — when the appointed hour passed without incident.

47. The Royal Yacht off St Michael's Mount during the coastal cruise of 1846, when Queen Victoria visited the island, obligingly leaving an imprint of her foot as she stepped ashore from her barge. St Michael's Mount has long played host to royalty visiting the area.

48. Dolly Pentreath's monument, incorporated in the wall of Paul churchyard, was erected by 'The Prince Louis Lucien Bonaparte in union with the Rev'd John Garrett' in June 1860. Although Dolly Pentreath has gone down in popular folklore as the last speaker of the Cornish language, this claim has been widely contested.

49. The Quay Fair, traditionally held on Midsummer Day, attracted folk from a wide rural area. After eating, drinking and enjoying all the fun of the fair, revellers rounded off a good day out with boat trips round Mount's Bay.

50. The Royal Baths Boarding and Lodging House, demolished towards the end of the last century, enjoyed the prestige of possessing hot and cold baths. All the water had to be heated and carried up to the bedrooms by hand. Saturday night was bath night.

51. This area of Wherrytown near the former Cafe Marina and *Beachfield Hotel*, which was once duneland where sand was excavated, has taken many a battering by storm. Here local folk are seen surveying the ravages of the 1895 storm.

52. The *Duke of Cumberland Inn* splendidly bedecked for the Diamond Jubilee celebrations of 1897.

53. The future Edward VII visited the area as the Prince of Wales in 1865 with the Princess, who became Queen Alexandra, and he paid a return visit on 9 April 1902 as monarch, coming ashore from a cruise. Here the folk of Penzance demonstrate their loyalty to the Crown.

54. The fleet in Mount's Bay creates an impressive spectacle in 1904. In July 1910 nearly two hundred warships which arrived for a ceremonial review by King George V had to disperse for safety reasons when a severe gale blew up, and the event was abandoned.

55. The design of *Truelove*, constructed from old floorboards by Mr. Ellis in 1906, was determined by the size and shape of his backyard. Neighbouring walls were demolished en route to get her launched. Having sailed once across Mount's Bay, she was pronounced unseaworthy by the Board of Trade, and beached at Eastern Green to become an object of curiosity.

56. On 1 July 1911, a large school of bottle-nosed whales became stranded on the beach, attracting much attention. Sadly, most of them died. There was great indignation when some callous people shot and disembowelled them in pursuit of trophies.

57. The National Union of Women's Suffrage Societies, a non-party, non-militant breakaway group from the W.S.P.U., passes through Penzance on its way from Land's End to London just before the outbreak of the First World War.

58. The Genatosan staff outing on 2 September 1919, when over 100 people enjoyed the post-war delights of a trip to Newquay. At that time, before the mass ownership of cars, it was customary for employers to organise annual excursions for their workers.

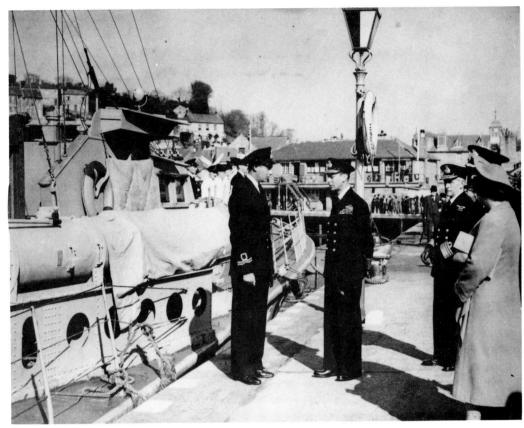

59. In 1942 King George VI and Queen Elizabeth made a morale-boosting visit to Newlyn. The royal couple then travelled on to South Crofty mine, Camborne, Redruth, Truro and Falmouth.

60. A spectacular sight at Mousehole in 1935 when the harbour crane was harnessed as an outsize fishing rod to land a 20-foot shark, tail first. The hooked shark dwarfs the nearer rowing boat and its occupants.

61. The Cafe Marina, situated at the western end of the Promenade, was a much-loved institution. In the 1920s and 1930s, smart young men hoping to cut a dash would take their young ladies there for a sedate cup of coffee or an ice cream. Unfortunately it was destroyed by fire in the 1930s.

62. Diluting the gravy outside Pool's Garage, Long Rock, during floods in the late 1930s. Quick to adapt to a situation, some local children prepare to cross the street in a rowing boat.

63.   Following the bureaucratic threat to the fishermen's homes, the Newlyn long liner *Rosebud* sailed around to the Houses of Parliament amidst a blaze of publicity to hand in a petition. *Rosebud* later performed wartime coastal service with the Royal Navy, returned to Newlyn and was renamed *Cynthia Yvonne.*

Views, Streets and Buildings

64. Construction work being carried out on St Mary's parish church in 1833, which occupies the site of the spired chapel of St Mary's, demolished in 1832.

65. This 1858 engraving of Penzance from the sea shows the church of St Mary's, a prominent navigational landmark, and the dome of the Market House.

66. View up Quay Street over a hundred years ago. The corner was re-aligned, the Harbour Office was demolished and a new one constructed near the centre foreground of this picture. During renovation work carried out earlier this century, a secret cupboard still containing two large, wooden kegs was discovered at the *Dolphin Hotel* (pictured here on the left).

67. View down Chapel Street, one of the most interesting and important streets in Penzance, which was formerly known as 'Our Lady Street'. It was the focus of Penzance life where theatrical performances, concerts and dances were held. In the middle of the photograph is the former home of Maria Branwell, who married Patrick Brontë and became the mother of the literary Brontë sisters.

68. Penzance, reputed to be as warm as Madrid, Florence and Constantinople in January with its Gulf Stream influence, rather fell down on its reputation in the winter of 1895 when the place took on a gleaming, white, petrified beauty, and even the fountains in the gardens froze in spectacular mid-jet.

69. An 1895 guidebook proclaimed: 'THE QUEEN'S ... (on the Esplanade facing due south)
Patronised by her Majesty the Queen of Holland and Prince Albrecht of Prussia ...', being 'The
Principal and Largest' comfortably furnished and with apartments en suite for 'Families, Ladies
and Gentlemen only'. There were Ladies', Drawing, Reading, Coffee, Smoking and Billiard Rooms,
while an hotel omnibus met every train entering the town.

70. Fashionable folk taking a leisurely stroll in Morrab Gardens amidst sub-tropical
vegetation. A guidebook of 1865 proclaimed: 'Winter is here deprived of its terrors
and summer is never oppressive. For these reasons a residence in Penzance is so often
prescribed to persons suffering under pulmonary complaints'.

71. In Newlyn, the fishermen's homes, close to the water and with cellars and scope for drying nets, were ideally suited to their way of life. It was the ultimate indignity when their much-loved houses were threatened by bureaucratic slum clearance in the late 1930s. Despite heartfelt protests, the scheme went ahead until halted by the Second World War.

72. Trewarveneth Street, Newlyn, in an area where contented cats sit on walls or lie in the sun, has changed little since this photograph was taken around the turn of the century. The delightful Rue des Beaux Arts (a name dreamed up by the Newlyn artists) leads off this street.

73. The 15th-century Manor House of the Keigwin Estate was the only building left standing in Mousehole after the devastating Spanish attack of 1595. Jenkin Keigwin was reputedly killed here by a cannon ball as he sought to defend the place.

74. The menfolk of Marazion pose for the photographer towards the end of the last century. Marazion, described by the historian Leland as a 'great long town', was formerly known as Market Jew.

Marazion. The Main Street.

75.   An early, motorised bus passes through The Square in Marazion in the days before the 'Parking Prohibited' notice there was necessary. Beyond is the old Town Hall clocktower on the site of the old Market House, and the *Marazion Hotel*, which is now the *Cutty Sark Hotel*.

76.   The entrance to St Michael's Mount. In the last century this village, at the base of the Mount, had three schools, a Wesleyan chapel, a customs house, a shop, a bakery and an inn. There were stables and a coach house and, before the underground railway was built, packhorses hauled up supplies for the castle.

Entrance to St. Michael's Mount.

77. Landward view from St Michael's Mount showing the Causeway and the Cross. The first Archpriest William Morton, who was responsible for constructing the early stone Causeway, was assisted by the Bishop of Exeter, who urged sinners to contribute — as an act of atonement. At high tide the Mount is accessible only by boat.

78. An atmospheric picture of St Michael's Mount.

St. Michaels Mount.

79. Gulval church, beautifully situated, bears many memorials to the influential Bolitho family. Its evocative and interesting churchyard contains the intriguing 18th-century pirate's grave, surrounded by romance and mystery.

80. The foundation stone of the Public Buildings in Penzance was laid on 27 April 1864, and the building, constructed of Lamorna granite, was opened three years later. The western wing houses the Royal Geological Society of Cornwall, a distinguished institution founded in 1814, which played an important part in the cultural and scientific life of the county.

81. (*opposite above*) A corner of The Greenmarket, as it looked in 1895. Shakerley the Chemist and Druggist is on the corner, while to the left is the former Chudleigh's, a popular eating place.

82. (*opposite below*) The same view westwards from the top of the Market House about 40 years on.

83. (*above*) This house in Alverton Road, now known as Hawk's Farm, was formerly the home of young Edward Pellew, an adventurous lad destined to achieve patriotic fame and glory, who became Admiral Pellew. The name 'Alverton' was derived from Alwardus, lord of the district in the days of Edward the Confessor.

84. (*below*) Looking up Market Jew Street, *c.*1900, with the statue of Sir Humphry Davy (1778-1829), the town's most illustrious son, outside the impressive east face of the Market House. This area was the busy hub of Penzance life, crammed with stalls and colourful awnings, with traders crying their wares. The railings were emplaced in 1864 for safety reasons.

Penzance, Market Jew Street.

85.   Demolition near the junction of Market Jew Street, Adelaide Street and Albert Street around the turn of the century, with just one vehicle in sight on the road to Chyandour. Today, this area, much changed, has become a bottleneck junction.

86.   The Pavilion on the Penzance seafront, built in 1911, provided stylish holiday entertainment with a restaurant, theatre and ballroom. During the Second World War concert parties were held here to 'beat those black-out blues'. The domes have now been replaced and it functions today as a leisure centre, offering videos, amusements, refreshments and a casino.

87. The Market House, pictured before the west face was remodelled, was designed by William Harris of Bristol and built in 1836. It replaced the earlier Market House, constructed in 1614 when Penzance achieved Borough status.

88. Renovation work was carried out on the Market House when Lloyd's Bank was established here in 1925. The west side was taken back and remodelled, replacing straight contours with the familiar curved walls of today. Alterations were also made to the fine dome.

89. Nursemaids and folk in their Sunday best take a sedate stroll along the Promenade past the prestigious *Queen's Hotel*, which has now lost its tower and entrance porch, but gained a modern face-lift.

90. Folk going about their everyday affairs in a picturesque corner of Coinagehall Street around 1930. Two young scholars share one of the lower of Paunch's Upper Steps, which led through to Quay Street. Today this area is much changed.

91. Folly House, pictured here in the 1930s, was for many years the oldest house in Penzance. It was demolished in the 1950s. The town, burnt by the Spaniards in 1595 and sacked by Fairfax, retained few buildings of antiquity.

92. The remarkable Egyptian House in Chapel Street was built in 1835/6 by John Lavin, a Penzance mineralogist, who occupied the place for some years. This was a progression from the building of the Classical School in Devonport in 1832, designed in a similar Egyptian style. Today it functions as a National Trust shop.

ALEXANDRA GARDENS AND TERRACE, PENZANCE.

93.   This is how the seafront gardens and The Terrace looked before the relentless storm of
1962 turned the fore-ground into rubble. It has now been reconstructed as a children's play
area, but the attractive footbridge has not been replaced. There are alterations on the seaward
side of the Bolitho Gardens, but the entrance (centre) appears much the same today.

94.   A terrific storm on 7 March 1962 reduced the lovingly-tended seafront gardens into a vast, impromptu rockery,
and created havoc all along the Penzance, Newlyn and Mousehole waterfront. Concrete was smashed, lamp
standards and railings torn down, houses were flooded and boats were set adrift. Despite all the devastation, no lives
were lost.

People

95. An old family barge, constructed on the Mount in the mid-18th century, was used for special occasions, when Lord St Levan's boatmen donned their distinctive livery, comprising leather caps bearing the family crest, and red watermen's coats worn over frilly shirts and white sea petticoats. The impressive brass badge worn on the left sleeve carried the St Aubyn arms.

96. Dolly Pentreath, a native of Mousehole who died in 1777, claimed to be the last person to speak the Cornish language. There is a revival of interest in the language, which is similar to Welsh, but more closely resembles Breton (see no. 48).

97. At the age of 84, Mary Kelynack of Newlyn became a celebrity after walking to London to the Great Fisheries Exhibition of 1851 with a cowal on her head, to draw attention to a financial matter. Her spirited exploit captured the imagination of the press, endeared her to the Lord Mayor and Lady Mayoress and touched the heart of Queen Victoria.

98. The staff of the *Union Hotel* in Chapel Street looking trim in their immaculate uniforms, *c.*1885. This hotel, built on the site of the old *Ship and Castle*, was the principal hotel in town in the early 19th century. The news of the victory at Trafalgar and Nelson's death was first announced here.

99. The arrival of General Booth, founder of the Salvation Army, at Penzance in 1890, where he was welcomed by officials and a crowd of enthusiastic followers at the railway station.

100. Floral names, long skirts, frills and large, extravagant hats supporting a variety of flowers, fruit and foliage were in vogue around Penzance, as in other parts of the country, at the turn of the century.

101. Children in their Sunday best, c.1905.

102. A team of well-organised gardeners pause with hoe, birch-broom and rake by the shrubbery in Morrab Gardens before the First World War.

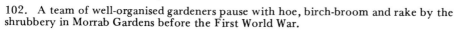

103. Lads at the fairground, *c.*1930.

104. Eye-catching fashions at the Mickey Mouse stall, where it is 'in for a penny ... in for a pound'.

105. Jimmy Chinn, the Cornish Boxing Champion 1929/30, poses in his gear for a studio shot against the romantic backcloth of a sylvan setting.

106.   The Yglesias sisters tending a patient at their bird hospital and sanctuary at Mousehole. Dorothy and Phyllis (Pog), who first came to the area on holiday in 1912 and became enchanted with the place, moved here in 1925 and devoted their lives to this work. Miss Dorothy Yglesias died in 1980, shortly before she was due to receive an MBE at Buckingham Palace.

107. Emperor Haile Selassie of Ethiopia on a visit to his daughter at St Clare's School, Penzance, in the mid-1930s.

Art and Inspiration

108. Fisherfolk by the cliff, Newlyn, have time for reflection while the nets dry out. Although only about a mile from Penzance, Newlyn has a totally different identity. It was the first Cornish place to attract a colony of artists, towards the end of the last century. They built up a good rapport with local folk.

109. The sight of fishing vessels leaving and entering Newlyn was a moving experience. Scenes such as this provided inspiration for the painters who colonised the place.

110. The 'Fathers' of the Newlyn Art Colony, c.1884. The colony, attracted here by the particular quality of the light and picturesque work-a-day life, became part of the local scene. Pictured here are: (standing, left to right) Frank Bodilly, Fred Millard, Frank Bramley, William Blandford Fletcher, William Breakespeare, Ralph Todd, Alexander Chevalier Tayler, Henry Scott Tuke. (Seated) William Wainwright, Edwin Harris and Stanhope Forbes.

111. As the area became the focus for artists and the visiting smart set, colourful local characters grasped new opportunities, as this well-known Mousehole guide demonstrates.

112. Staff of the Newlyn Fisheries
Exhibition pose for the photographer
in an engaging array of bonnets and
aprons, amidst the baskets, nets and
ropes of their trade.

113. Betsy Lanyon and Blanche
Courtney posing as models in this
studio study, wearing the clothes of
their trade amidst their tackle, and
in front of a painted backdrop. The
heavy weight of fish baskets was
supported by horsehair pads worn
around the waist, offset by brow-
bands.

114. This delightful study captures the scenic romantic charm associated with Old Newlyn. Fishermen and bathing boys were the particular inspiration for the paintings of Stanhope Forbes and H. S. Tuke.

115. Local folk, used to posing as decorative models, pause for the photographer in Jenny Lind Court at Newlyn, around the turn of the century.

116. Everyday life in Newlyn, with its steep, narrow cobbled streets and open doorways, had a picturesque quality, appreciated by the artists. Even washing day, depicted here, had a certain poetic charm.

117. Dame Laura Knight spent a happy, creative period in Cornwall between 1907 and 1918, when her work blossomed. She successfully captured the spirit of the place, and her work reflected her happiness.

THEATRE PENZANCE.

By Permission of the Worshipful the Mayor.

ON MONDAY EVENING, SEPTEMBER 15, 1828,

Will be presented a much admired new petit COMEDY, in two Acts, as performed at the English Opera House, with the greatest approbation, called the

CORNISH MINERS.

Hubert Kynan *(a Master Miner)*	Mr. MILLER
Stephen Kynan *(his Son)*	Mr. HOWARD
Trevallion	Mr. A. DAWSON
Engineer	Mr. DAWSON
Sal Ammo *(a Village Doctor)*	Mr. J. DAWSON
Githian *(a Maniac)*	Mr. MAY
Bobby Redruth *(a Miner)*	Mr. DAWSON
Dame Kynan	Mrs. J. DAWSON
Jane Oswald	Miss FRY
Anne Oswald	Mrs. CHAPMAN

Villagers, Old Women, Miners, &c. &c.

In Act 1.—The Interior of Dame Oswald's Cottage.

SCENE 3.—THE SHAFT, OR ENTRANCE OF THE MINE.

Scene 4.—INTERIOR of a TIN MINE.

ACT 2. SCENE 3.—GALLERY IN THE MINE.

SCENE 4.

The Maniac's Den in the Mine.

Comic Song by Mr. J. Dawson.

A SONG BY MR. MILLER.

To which will be added, the favourite Comic Farce, in 3 Acts, called the

MIDNIGHT HOUR;

Or, the War of Wits.

GENERAL	Mr. DAWSON
MARQUIS	Mr. HOWARD
SEBASTIAN	Mr. A. DAWSON
MATTHIAS	Mr. MILLER
NICHOLAS	Mr. J. DAWSON
DUENNA	Mrs. DAWSON
JULIA	Miss FRY
FLORA	Mrs. CHAPMAN

In Rehearsal, and Speedily will be Produced,

GIL BLAS,——DUMB GIRL,——OBI, &c.

Doors open at 6 and begin at 7 o'clock.—Half Price commences about half past 8

Boxes, 3s.—Pit, 1s. 6d.—Gallery 1s.—Half Price, Boxes, 2s.—Pit 1s.—Gallery 6d.

BOX PLACES AND TICKETS TO BE HAD OF Mr. VIGURS.

VIGURS, PRINTER AND BOOKBINDER, PENZANCE.

118. Behind the *Union Hotel* in Chapel Street is the second oldest theatre in the county, which operated from 1787 to 1831 and attracted well-known actors of the time. It was well situated over a stable in the yard, and performances were sometimes enlivened by unscheduled sound and scent effects off stage. This playbill dates from 1828.

119. Newlyn Old Fair in the 1890s, with its lively and distinctive brand of fairground art and hand-held placards proclaiming an array of diverse attractions and curiosities, including the Fat Lady.

120. W. C. & S. Hancock's motor car switchback, with its 87-key Gavioli organ, was a masterpiece of fairground technology. There was great excitement when the fair came to town at Corpus Christi. This photograph was taken in 1902.

121. Stylish socialising on Treglown's Picnic Grounds, Marazion, at the beginning of the century.

122. Bathing machines for ladies and gentlemen, suitably distanced from each other, were drawn up and down the beach by ponies, according to the tide, to allow bathers to enter the water with suitable decorum.

123. This delightful photographic study captures the childhood magic of the traditional seaside holiday, 1927 style.

124. Local folk enjoying the age-old, exhilarating game of dodge-the-spray, as rough seas pound the Promenade around 1914. However, a bigger storm was brewing at the time as warships and reservists were being summoned to Portsmouth.

125. Penzance Rifle Volunteers, in an array of outfits, looking in all directions as the photographer takes aim and fires the shutter. The Rifle Band provided music for a variety of colourful local events. For many years their headquarters was in the Corn Exchange at the Guildhall.

126. Members, many of them founder members, of the Penzance Independent Brass Band, with their conductor Mr. John Andrew. This band, consisting of teetotallers, was proud of having won more prizes than any other Cornish band.

127. The men of Penzance, in an array of arresting swimwear, at the indoor swimming baths around 1930.

Recollections of War

128.   This engraving by William Willis, dating from about 1860, shows the view from Newlyn Battery towards Penzance where another battery emplaced on the rocks can be seen. St Michael's Mount has always formed a natural fortress in times of war. Mount's Bay witnessed many a skirmish in Napoleonic times.

129.   A triumphal arch to honour the 2nd Duke of Cornwall's Light Infantry's engagements of 1882 and 1885/6 around Dettingen, Dominica, Sevastopol, Lucknow and the Nile. Some spectators take advantage of the roof of the railway station to improve their view.

130. The unveiling of this memorial in the Morrab Gardens to the men of Penzance who lost their lives in the South African War (1899-1902) took place on Saturday 5 November 1904 in the presence of the Mayor, Aldermen, Councillors, Officers and Men of the Artillery and Rifle Volunteers. The singing of 'Onward Christian Soldiers' followed a prayer.

131. Penzance Military Band pictured just before the First World War.

132. (*above*) The Navy League was well supported in Penzance. In 1914 the Committee demanded that the government 'shall lay down 6 large ships every year until 1918, thus maintaining superiority at the rate of 2 keels to 1, as in this way only can Great Britain's superiority remain in the prominent position the Empire stands in at the present moment'.

133. (*below*) During the First World War Penzance became an Auxiliary Naval Base, with Holman's offices the headquarters for naval personnel. The workforce and facilities were harnessed for the war effort. After the war the firm was reimbursed for resultant wear and tear.

134. (*opposite above*) Service personnel aboard R.M.S. *Lapwing* leaving Penzance Harbour around the beginning of the First World War.

135. (*opposite below*) R.M.S. *Peninnis* preparing to enter dry dock on the tide. Built as the coastguard cutter *Argus* in 1904, she was taken over as a wartime Naval patrol vessel and renamed *Argon*. After the war she was renovated and renamed *Peninnis*, and served on the Penzance-Scillies run for six years. She was sold in 1927 and broken up in 1932.

136. R.M.S. *Lyonesse*, pictured here in 1908, carried early flowers and vegetables for mainline markets. In March 1915 she picked up 94 survivors from the British steamers *Indian City*, *Andalusian* and *Headlands*, which had been torpedoed by German submarine U29. Despite great efforts, *Headlands*, which was later taken in tow, sank after 3 hours.

137. *The Cornishman* of 11 November 1918 carried a headline: 'PEACE ... Germany Signs Armistice ... The Last Shot Fired...'. On Armistice Day the Union flag was much in evidence and Mount's Bay re-echoed to a jubilant cacophony of ships' sirens. There were Peace Parades to celebrate the end of the conflict. This photograph shows soldiers parading at St Clare Cricket Ground.

138. With the coming of peace, a triumphal arch was erected at Wherrytown to honour the heroes of the three armed services at the end of the First World War. Christmas 1918 was expected to go down in history as 'The Peace Christmas'.

SERMAN SUBMARINE
ENTERING PENZANCE DOCK

139. (*overleaf*) Lowestoft masts and funnels alongside the pier at Newlyn in the 1930s. At the outbreak of war many vessels were requisitioned by the authorities, and experienced crews manned them. Deep-sea vessels such as these fished with the protection of escorts. Towards the end of the war fishermen appealed for the speedy return of their boats, vital to their livelihooods.

140. (*above*) An ex-German submarine brought into Penzance Dock on 3 January 1919 was opened to the visiting public, which was urged to resist the temptation to make off with souvenirs.

141. (*below*) A War Memorial, in the form of an obelisk, was constructed on the site of the 18th-century battery, and unveiled on 14 May 1922. It was placed in a prominent position so that future generations would never forget the dead of the First World War.

142. An aerial view of Penzance, taken about 1938. It shows Jubilee Bathing Pool, constructed in 1935, which became an armed camp in the Second World War, with gun emplacements and searchlights for the surveillance of Mount's Bay. The area around the pool and St Anthony's Gardens was inaccessible to the public. High cross-scaffolding and barbed wire cut off the mined foreshore.

143. A gas decontamination squad awaiting orders outside the Police Station during a 1939 A.R.P. drill. Their strenuous task would be to wash down areas contaminated by liquid gas. Masks were removed outside the area. Danger of fumes adhering to oilskins meant three washing routines before they were allowed to change into fresh clothes and take a rest.

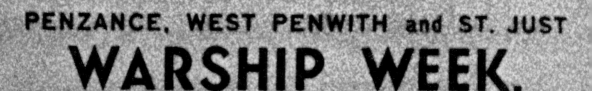

PENZANCE, WEST PENWITH and ST. JUST
WARSHIP WEEK.
22nd—29th November.
Chairman: HIS WORSHIP THE MAYOR OF PENZANCE.

WEEK'S OBJECTIVE - £210,000.
Cost of the HULL of the Destroyer H.M.S "WITCH."

SATURDAY, 3.0 P.M., GRAND OPENING.
(For full particulars, see Thursday's "Tidings.")

144. (*overleaf*) Volunteers digging tank traps on Eastern Green at the beginning of the Second World War. The old signal box can be seen to the right of the picture.

145. (*above*) Special fund-raising activities were held throughout the war. 'Don't keep your money in a teapot or sewn up in your skirt', declared Col. E. H. W. Bolitho, Lord Lieutenant of Cornwall, during Warship Week, November 1941. 'The teapot may get broken or the skirt lost!' A naval representative added, 'It's better to be broke than broken'.

146. Just after the Second World War, the battleship, H.M.S. *Warspite*, which had seen active service, broke her tow lines in Mount's Bay and became stranded on the shore at Prussia Cove as she was being towed to the breaker's yard in South Wales. In this incident, the Penlee lifeboat crew was honoured for carrying out heroic rescue work, and Coxswain Madron received the Silver Medal.

147. The Newlyn Fire Service pictured during the Second World War behind St John's Hall, Penzance. The combined defence services were put through their paces in the early part of the war, carrying out simulated emergencies.

148. Members of the National Fire Service pictured outside St John's Hall around 1942.

149.   Newlyn Fireman Jack Tonkin beside the immaculate No. 1 National Fire Service vehicle which carried breathing apparatus along with its extending ladder on the roof. The Fire Service was based close by the Magpie Soccer Club.

Wreck and Rescue

150.   Launching one of Penzance's early self-righting, pulling and sailing lifeboats (c.1895-1913) from the old lifeboat house in Wharf Road. In an emergency the Coxswain rang the bell in the turret, while the Hon. Secretary alerted the Job Master, who roused the four horses stabled in Chapel Street, put on their tackle and contacted the drivers.

151. The lifeboat *Elizabeth and Blanche* with her Newlyn crew wearing cork and kapok lifejackets, *c.*1908. This Watson-type lifeboat, the second to bear that name, was placed on station in 1899. She was transferred to Newlyn Harbour, where launching was easier, in 1908, prior to the building of Penlee Lifeboat Station, midway between Newlyn and Mousehole in 1912/13.

152. The Isles of Scilly packet steamer, *Lady of the Isles*, beached off Lamorna Pier after striking a reef in 1904.
Built by Harvey's of Hayle, she came into service in 1875 and subsequently took part in many salvage operations
around these treacherous coasts. She was mined off Falmouth on 3 October 1940, while on Admiralty service.

PENLEE LIFEBOAT

153. A lifeboat being launched from Penlee Lifeboat Station, *c.*1929. On the fateful night of 19 December 1981,
the lifeboat *Solomon Browne*, manned by her brave crew of eight, in appalling conditions went down this slipway
for the last time, aiming to preserve life from shipwreck. The tragic events which followed made worldwide
news and immortalised the crew as heroes of the sea.

Postscript

154.   After 360 years of corporate
existence, with expansion in 1934,
Penzance lost its Borough status in
1974, to become part of the County
District of Penwith. The new town
badge is shown as illustrated on the
New Letters Patent. (Reproduced
by courtesy of Penzance Town
Council)

Bibliography

Barton, R. M., *Life in Cornwall in the mid-Nineteenth Century*, 1971.
Barton, R. M., *Life in Cornwall in the late Nineteenth Century*, 1972.
Barton, R. M., *Life in Cornwall at the end of the Nineteenth Century*, 1974.
Batten, Ben, *Newlyn Boyhood*.
Batten, Ben, *Newlyn Heritage*, 1980.
Batten, Ben, *Newlyn Towners, Fishermen and Methodists*.
Corin, John, and Farr, Grahame, *Penlee Lifeboat*, 1983.
Corin, John, and Farr, Grahame, *R.N.L.I. Penlee*.
Farr, Grahame, *Wreck and Rescue Round the Cornish Coast*, 1965.
Farr, Grahame, *West Country Passenger Steamers*, 1967.
Folliott Stokes, A. G., *From Land's End to The Lizard*, 1909.
Laws, Peter, *The Industries of Penzance*, 1978.
Noall, Cyril, and Williams, Douglas, *The Book of Penzance*, 1983
Pool, P. A. S., *The History of the Town and Borough of Penzance*.
Mais, S. P. B., *The Cornish Riviera*, 1929.
Murray, John, *Hand Book: Devon and South Cornwall*, 1865.
Rees, Edgar A., *Old Penzance*, 1956.
Roddis, Roland, *Cornish Harbours*, 1951.
Salmon, Arthur L., *The Heart of the West*.
Soulsby, Ian, *A History of Cornwall*, 1986.
St Aubyn, John, *St Michael's Mount*, 1974.
Ward, C. S., and Baddeley, M. J. B., *Thorough Guide: South Devon and South Cornwall*, 1895.
Williams, Douglas, *Mount's Bay*, 1984.

Other sources

Guide to Penzance, Ward Lock & Company Ltd., London and Melbourne.
'Rescue 21': Penlee and Penzance Branch of the R.N.L.I. and The Lions Club of Penzance, 1981.
The Cornishman and Cornish Telegraph newspaper.